Ann Su...

Creator of the ...mous
Bakewell Pudding

Centuries of family history in and around the town of Bakewell

Paul Hudson

Ann Summers Creator of the World Famous Bakewell Pudding

Paul Hudson

Published by
Pynot Publishing
56 Main Road
Holmesfield
Dronfield
Derbyshire
S18 7WT
England

Tel & Fax: 0114 289 0348
Email: info@pynotpublishing.co.uk

Find us on the World Wide Web at www.pynotpublishing.co.uk

First Published 2008

Printed and bound in the United Kingdom by Polestar-Wheatons, Exeter.

ISBN 978-0-9552251-7-8

CONTENTS

INTRODUCTION

What was it like in the late 1940s being brought up in an historic market town of roughly 3,000 inhabitants like Bakewell, born into a family steeped in local traditions? Vaguely remembering stories told by my grandparents, parents, uncles, aunties and cousins about family ties with George Stephenson, the railway pioneer; Sir Joseph Paxton, the Bachelor Duke of Devonshire's Head Gardener at Chatsworth House, designer of The Crystal Palace and Member of Parliament; Sir Humphry Davy, the leading scientist of the 1800s; and Mrs Ann Greaves, the originator of the world famous Bakewell Pudding? Water off a duck's back, I suppose! Were they really relatives or just closely connected with the lives of my ancestors? So many family stories with no great detail, muddled but full of events. Clouded in my mind, tales occasionally recounted at family gatherings. Listening in to adults chatting. Trying to separate fact from fiction. So many of the people to whom we were introduced when I was young seemed to me to be important, always to be respected! Why didn't I ask more questions at the time?

The Rutland Arms Hotel in the 1800s. [Hudson Collection]

The Rutland Arms Hotel, Bakewell. Standing proud and tall overlooking Rutland Square in the town centre, taken for granted most of the time – it had always been there. The Rutland was where, as a child dressed in best clothes, my parents took me for birthday meals; where my Dad, Gill Hudson, who was the General Manager of Bakewell's DP Battery Company, entertained his business clients; where I first donned a dinner jacket and joined my family at the annual Red Cross Ball; where my sister, Jane, held her wedding reception; where my wife, Jan, and I met for a quick drink before we walked across The Square to the Town Hall to be married; where we fed and watered the mourners after the funerals of my Mum and Dad.

Jan & I crossing Rutland Square on our way from The Rutland to the Register Office in the Town Hall to get married – 20th February 1989. [Hudson Collection]

My enduring childhood memory of 'The Rutland', as it was known locally, is of my attempts, each crisp and often snowy Boxing Day, to wheedle my parents into allowing me to join an enormous crowd of Bakewell people watch the stirring sight of the High Peak Hunt. All its followers would gather in The Square outside the hotel before setting off into the surrounding hills for a day's sport. To see all the riders in their colourful clothes followed some way behind by the youngsters from the local Pony Club! The Hunt had taken its stirrup cup in The Square outside the hotel each year since the days when it was first formed in 1848.

The Rutland Arms had always been there but as a child nobody had told me of the close links between the hotel and the Hudson family. Many members of our family had been unaware that our great-great-great-grandfather, James Hudson, had been the first innkeeper of The Rutland during its construction back in 1803. He and my great-great-great-grandmother, Ann Hudson (later to become the renowned Mrs Greaves of Bakewell Pudding fame), had run the bustling coaching inn and posting house in its early days.

My elder brother, Roger, with ambitions to become an hotel manager, was given his first school holiday job at The Rutland Arms shovelling potatoes deep in the cellars. What history had surrounded him down there way beneath those mighty historic walls? Were the cellars those of the original White Horse that had stood on approximately the same site for several hundred years before The Rutland was built? I must mention that on occasions he was allowed out of the cellars to wash dishes in the kitchen! I am sure Roger would never have imagined that, in the fullness of time, after a successful career in hotel management, his final hotel before retirement would be the magnificent Peacock Hotel, three miles down the road from Bakewell at Rowsley; another establishment originally built for the Manners family, which at the time of writing, is back under their administration.

The licensed trade has always been near to the heart of the Hudson family and as the story of our family unfurls it will become apparent that hotels, inns and pubs have always played an important part in our history, one way or another!

Left: *An unusual angle of Haddon Hall painted in the 19th century.*
[Hudson Collection]

Below: *The entry in the Matlock Marriage Register for the wedding of James Hudson to Ann Summers, 29th October 1800.*

4

FROM ANN SUMMERS VIA ANN HUDSON TO ANN GREAVES ALL IN THE SHORT SPACE OF FIVE YEARS AND A DAY!

In 1778 my great-great-great-grandmother Ann Summers was born (no, I haven't been able to connect her with the family of the other Ann Summers, of High Street sex shops fame – yet!). She was born in the Derbyshire village of Swanwick, near Alfreton, where most of the inhabitants worked either in the iron works, down the coal mines, or were employed in the manufacture of silk stockings and footwear.

In June 1817 a large number of the villagers of Swanwick were heavily involved in the Pentrich Revolution, an armed struggle precipitated by the poor conditions and poverty amongst the numerous desperate soldiers and sailors who had recently returned to their communities virtually empty-handed after defeating Napoleon and his armies in Europe. What followed was a recession in the iron and textile industries. This 'Revolution' was the last occurrence in the history of England when an armed mob had attempted to march on London with the intention of bringing down the Government. Needless to say the 'Revolution' came to a hasty end when a detachment of the King's Hussars was deployed to quell the revolt.

Ann Summers would have grown up in the village with many of the 23 Swanwick men who were arrested by the army. Those found guilty were either sentenced to a term of imprisonment or transported to the colonies. The three ringleaders of the Pentrich Revolution were tried and found guilty of high treason. They were the last persons in England ever to be sentenced to be hanged, drawn and quartered. On this occasion, however, the Prince Regent, on behalf of his father, King George III, decreed that their punishment should be commuted to mere hanging and beheading! Small mercy! The sentence was carried out on Nun's Green in front of Derby Gaol.

Ann moved from Swanwick to the Matlock Bath area, possibly to find employment in the cotton mills or in one of the inns and there she met her intended, my great-great-great-grandfather, James Hudson. Perhaps he was already in the innkeeping trade? On 29th October 1800 at St Giles' Church in Matlock they were married in the presence of his parents, James and Mary Hudson, and another relative, Martha Hudson (see Matlock Marriage Register, opposite).

James and Ann probably lived near one of the three Arkwright cotton mills at Masson and Cromford because both their daughters were baptised at Sir Richard Arkwright's private chapel in the valley below his home at Willersley Castle near the River Derwent. That same chapel is now used as the parish church of St Mary, Cromford. Their daughters were Mary Hudson, born on 10th November 1801 and Ann Hudson, who was born in Matlock Bath on 19th March 1803.

In late 1803 the Hudson family moved to Bakewell where James became the licensee and innkeeper of the brand new Rutland Arms Inn. There he oversaw its construction whilst also farming several hundred acres of land at Haddon. The Rutland Arms Inn was built on the instructions of the landowner, the Duke of Rutland, as an attempt to rival the Duke of Devonshire's conversion of Buxton into a successful spa town. The inn was built in Market Place, as Rutland Square was known at that time, more or less on the site of the old White Horse Inn whose name was later transferred to the old stable buildings at the bottom end of South Church Street. This bar lived on well into the late twentieth century and many Bakewell locals will fondly remember it as the 'Blood-Tub' or the taproom of The Rutland next door. Sadly, the Blood-Tub closed for licensed business in the 1990s and, after a period as a patchwork business, the premises are empty at the time of writing.

James Hudson farmed several hundred acres around Haddon Hall as well as performing the role of Innkeeper of The Rutland. Haddon Hall was uninhabited for much of the eighteenth century and all of the nineteenth century. The Manners family seldom visited the lovely house and preferred to remain in their Leicestershire seat at Belvoir Castle. However, a ball was held in Haddon Hall in 1802 for the inhabitants of Bakewell on the occasion of the temporary peace in the war with France created by the Treaty of Amiens.

On 10th June 1804 at The Rutland, Ann Hudson gave birth to her third child, this time a son, James. He was baptised at All Saints Church in Bakewell. Tragically, less than a year after the birth of baby James, Ann's husband, James, died at the inn. He was only 29 years old, a relatively young age. The following day, on 19th April 1805, he was buried in Bakewell churchyard in a grave which can be found close to the south door of the church.

The licence of the Rutland Arms was swiftly transferred to his widow, Ann Hudson, to enable her to continue the business. James had died intestate so on 18th October 1805, in the forty-fifth year of the reign of King George III, Ann applied for and was granted letters of administration. She received advice and assistance in her application from two friends of the family, William Greaves – a plumber and glazier – and William Smith – a stonemason – both from Bakewell. The laws of inheritance at that time decreed that Ann would have only been entitled to one third of James' estate of around £1,000. £1,000 in 1805 would amount to approximately £100,000 in today's money but would probably have had more purchasing power. The remainder would have been put into trust for the benefit of the children and especially for his only son, James.

James' estate had included 12 post and saddle horses and harness, 2 husbandry horses and gearing, 2 cows, 102 sheep and 3 pigs. He had owned 3 post chaises, 3 carts and many implements of husbandry including plows (ploughs) and harrows. From the list of furniture for the several rooms in the building it is possible to imagine the layout of the interior of the Inn. There was a kitchen and scullery, a bar parlour, a taproom, three more parlours, a dining room, five chambers (the more comfortable bedrooms) and eight attick (attic) bedrooms to accommodate the servants of visitors and the staff of the Inn. In the cellars were 38 gallons of wine and varying amounts of brandy, rum, gin, ale and porter.

The sudden lack of funds may well have prompted Ann Hudson into rushing headlong into remarriage. On 30th October 1805, just six months and a few days after the death of her husband, James, only twelve days after her being granted letters of administration and just nine days after victory in the infamous Battle of Trafalgar, Ann married her plumber and glazier friend, William Greaves Jnr.

William was the second (and certainly not the last as we shall discover later!) William Greaves to have been born in Bakewell and baptised with that name. His grandfather, Joseph, had moved south to Bakewell from Wakefield in the early 1700s.

Ann and William's wedding ceremony was held at Bakewell Church and was witnessed by William's mother, Elizabeth, and his brother, Joseph. William Greaves became the licensee and innkeeper of the Rutland Arms and together with Ann ran the coaching inn for the next 26 years. In 1809 William also became the official postmaster for Bakewell with Ann as his deputy.

In the early years the stagecoaches had to struggle along the rough turnpikes. The journey from Matlock to Bakewell had been along the high ground through Hackney, Darley, Stancliffe and Northwood to Rowsley. Prior to 1759 the track had then crossed the River Derwent, turned north up Church Lane in Rowsley past what is now the Peacock Hotel and, after it had wound its way below Manners and Wicksop Woods, the turnpike entered Bakewell along Coombs Road and swept over single-tracked Bakewell Bridge into the centre of town.

Little by little, as landowners agreed to roads being carved through their land, the road system was improved and by 1762 the route from Rowsley to Bakewell was more or less the same as the A6 is today. The Duke of Rutland, although not being in full-time residence at Haddon Hall during the 1700s and 1800s, wanted the new road to pass to the west of the Hall and not to follow the old route along Coombs Road so he provided the finance for the whole project. The relatively narrow Fillyford Bridge carried the new turnpike over the River Wye near Pickory Corner. This bridge can still be seen over the wall in the fields a few yards north of the present A6 road. It is an attractive three-arch stone structure and it is a shame it is lost in the undergrowth.

Fillyford Bridge and the old turnpike crossing the River Wye at Pickory Corner, near Haddon Hall.
[Hudson Collection]

The route of the turnpike northwards from Bakewell would then have taken the high ground via Monsal Head and Wardlow Mires on its way to Buxton and the north. It was not until 1815 that a new road northwards from Bakewell was opened. This new road went along The Duke's Drive past Ashford-in-the-Water and cut through Taddington Dale to Taddington. Here the Waterloo Hotel was built at the side of the road to commemorate the famous victory over Napoleon that same year.

The Post Office mail coaches that used the route were each supervised by a heavily armed guard who sat alone on the mailbox dressed in the Post Office livery of scarlet and gold. He would be heavily armed with two pistols and a blunderbuss and amongst his responsibilities was the blowing of his coaching horn on approaching a tollgate. This warned the toll collector to open the gate to let the coach through without any delay to the Royal Mail. He would also blow his post horn to announce the arrival of the coach at a coaching inn where the horses would be changed. He carried an ancient timepiece to make sure the coach arrived on time.

A mail coach in 1827.

Tollhouses were built at intervals along the roads in order to collect fees from the travellers. These fees or tolls were supposed to be spent on the maintenance of the roads but instead were often spent on paying dividends to the shareholders. The streets in the town of Bakewell would more often that not have been covered with horse or cow muck forcing most of the gentry to travel on horseback or by carriage.

Ann Greaves gave birth to her second son, but her first and only child with new husband, William, in June 1807 and on the 22nd he was baptised William Greaves at All Saints Church in Bakewell.

Baby William, who was to be known throughout the family as 'Billy', his elder half-sisters, Mary Hudson and Ann Hudson, and half-brother, James Hudson, grew up in and around Bakewell. Although there was some difference in their ages they would probably have been educated together, first at home with a governess and later, in the case of James and Billy, at Lady Manners School. Here lessons were held in a cottage at the bottom of South Church Street just around the corner from the inn. They would have been taught English, Greek and Latin as well as Mathematics and Geography.

JANE AUSTEN
AND HER SOJOURN AT THE RUTLAND

Did Jane Austen stay at the Rutland Arms Inn when she was researching her novel, *Pride and Prejudice*? More people than not declare that she did and there is to this day a room at the hotel that bears her name. As Austen fans will know, Jane's father first presented the manuscript of the story of the Bingleys and the Bennets to Jane's publishers in 1797 under the title *First Impressions*. The publishers rejected it and Jane worked on the novel for sixteen more years until in 1813 *Pride and Prejudice* eventually went into print. It has proved to be a best seller ever since.

Jane Austen as her sister, Cassandra, saw her, from a sketch in 1810. [National Portrait Gallery]

Did Jane visit the inn when it was still the White Horse in the 1790s or, more likely, did she spend her time rewriting the novel looking out of the window of the Rutland Arms into The Square below, soaking up the atmosphere of this wonderful Peakland market town? The story that has circulated locally for many generations is that she did indeed stay at The Rutland in 1811 and I like to think that Ann Greaves and her staff looked after Jane Austen's every need at the inn and so do, I think, most Bakewell people.

Lord Byron, the poet, is also credited with a visit to The Rutland from his home at Newstead Abbey in Sherwood Forest just over the Nottinghamshire border. He also visited Matlock Bath and likened it to Switzerland, hence its nickname of 'Little Switzerland'.

On 29th June 1815 a daily return stagecoach route was inaugurated from Buxton via The Rutland Arms in Bakewell to the Old Bath Hotel in Matlock Bath. William Greaves had a team of excellent ostlers, farriers and horse-keepers for servicing the mail coaches and would have kept a selection of well over fifty horses to enable them to be changed regularly. During one week in 1818 no fewer than 655 coach passengers travelled through Bakewell. Seven or eight coaches a day would have stopped at the Rutland Arms to change horses and often to swap over coach drivers. A coachman's average day was fifty miles.

Lord George Gordon Byron as he appeared to painter, Richard Westall, in 1813. [National Portrait Gallery]

With roads improving the length of time for the coach journey from London to Manchester, via Bakewell, decreased. The 189 mile route would have passed through Edgware, St Albans, Luton, Bedford, Kettering, Market Harborough, Leicester, Loughborough, Derby, Matlock, Bakewell, Buxton, Stockport and on to Manchester. For those locals who can remember the days of the London Midland & Scottish Railway, the names of the stops are reminiscent of the station names on the London to Manchester via Bakewell railway line that so many of us enjoyed and now fondly miss. The total time for the journey from London to Manchester by stagecoach was just 21 hours.

From 1838 Bakewell had a daily post from London. The mailcoaches continued to run between Matlock and Manchester until October 1858.

An engraving of Chatsworth House from the south-west after the Bachelor Duke's alterations.

'MAD' KING GEORGE IS SUCCEEDED BY THE PRINCE REGENT, 1820

William Greaves was a religious man and a pillar of Bakewell society. He was shown on the 1824 list of members of Bakewell parish church as owning his own pew *"for the sole use of his family"*.

The young James Hudson was already in London finishing his education and looking for his first job. I often wonder how James prepared himself for life in London. Did he go to university? Did he have a job in Bakewell before venturing south? Did he have a strong Derbyshire accent? How will we ever know?

James came from that extraordinary era when young men achieved and were given tremendous responsibility at a surprisingly early age. Not many years earlier William Pitt the Younger had entered Cambridge University at the age of 14, become Chancellor of the Exchequer at 23 and Prime Minister at 24; Isaac Newton had become a revolutionary scientist at 25; Henry Fielding's plays were being performed in London when he was just 21; Mozart had completed several tours of Europe performing his famous orchestral works at the age of 15 and Joseph Paxton had become Head Gardener to the Duke of Devonshire at Chatsworth House at 22. James' inheritance from his father had obviously been spent well on his education.

On 9th March 1826, at the surprisingly young age of 21, James was appointed Assistant Secretary and Librarian of the Royal Society in London. The Royal Society first came into being in November 1660 and was intended *"for the promoting of*

Church of St Mary-le-Strand and the Strand front of Somerset House in 1836.
The rooms used by The Royal Society are to the left of the three arches.

experimental learning". By 1826 it was based at Somerset House in The Strand, Westminster, and James had an apartment there. His post required a good working knowledge of the general sciences, modern languages, Greek and Latin. As the curator of experiments he would have been a professional scientist and analogous to being an Oxford or Cambridge professor in the period.

Sir Humphry Davy, c1821, the President of The Royal Society at the time that James Hudson was appointed Assistant Secretary and Librarian. [National Portrait Gallery]

The President of the Royal Society at the time of his appointment was Sir Humphry Davy, the world famous scientist. James was later to serve two more Presidents, Mr Davies Gilbert and HRH Prince Augustus Frederick – the Duke of Sussex and sixth son of King George III. James Hudson worked with Davy and his assistant, Michael Faraday, on numerous scientific experiments.

In an extract from *The Library and Archives of the Royal Society 1660-1990* by Marie Boas Hall, we learn:

> *"As Assistant Secretary, Hudson was also Librarian and presumably Housekeeper and very much the servant of the Council, whose permission he had to ask when he wished to marry. This was at least partly so that the Council could make it clear that his widow would have no claim on the Society, partly so that she could be inspected to ascertain if she could act as Housekeeper."*

After having presented his future wife to the Council for 'inspection', which she obviously passed, James was given permission to marry Mary Denham, the eldest daughter of Mr Read Denham of Calow, Chesterfield. The wedding was held at St Mary & All Saints Church, Chesterfield, on 2nd January 1827.

Michael Faraday in 1831, an expert in electromagnetism and electrochemistry who worked closely with James Hudson. [National Portrait Gallery]

Just one month after James and Mary's wedding, Ann Greaves and her husband, William, would have had to travel all the way to London by stagecoach to attend another family wedding. This time the marriage of her younger daughter, Ann Hudson, to George Bradley, a solicitor. The wedding took place on 7th February 1827 in the Church of St Dunstan in the West in Fleet Street, London, very close to the Inns of Court. The church at that time would have been the original 13th century church that jutted out into the centre of Fleet Street and not the present 1829 Gothic revival version. James Hudson and his new wife, Mary, would have walked the few hundred yards to the wedding from their home at Somerset House. Perhaps the newly wed Ann Bradley had met her new husband during a visit to London to see her brother, James. The witnesses at the wedding were the bride's stepfather, William Greaves, her sister, Mary Hudson and Mary's fiance, McKay Balmannie.

Elder sister, Mary Hudson, later married McKay Balmannie and probably emigrated to the United States of America where her son, Alex, was born in 1830.

The period that James Hudson was associated with the Royal Society was one of the most exciting times in the rapid progression of scientific discovery. In an extract from the Committee Book of the Royal Society, dated 26th April 1827, in a report to the General Committee of the Board of Longitude and Royal Society for the Manufacture of Glass for Optical Purposes, the Secretary of the Royal Society, Sir John Frederick William Herschel, wrote:

"In the Former Experiments the Diligent Attendance and Active Assistance of Mr Hudson was of the Highest Utility in this respect: and they cannot help attributing a considerable portion of the Success which attended those First Trials, to his constant presence on the spot, his continual communication with his Employers, and his Zealous Discharge of his Duty, as an Operator."

During the above experiments James Hudson had worked closely with the project leader, Michael Faraday.

Sir John Frederick William Herschel in 1835, the mathematician, astronomer, chemist and experimental photographer who praised James Hudson for his work on the manufacture of optical glass. [National Portrait Gallery]

The President of the Royal Society, who originally encouraged James to apply for the job, was Sir Humphry Davy. By the middle of 1827 Davy was very ill and thought to be suffering from the effects of the inhalation of gases over the years during the many scientific experiments he had performed. He travelled to Europe in the hope of recovery but during his vacation he decided to resign from the position of President. As can be seen in the following letter of resignation sent to Mr Davies Gilbert, who at that time was Vice-President of the Royal Society, Sir Humphry seemed so concerned about the condition of his haemorrhoids and the inefficiency of the Austrian postal service that he almost forgot to tender his resignation! In the postscript he enquired about James Hudson's current position at the Royal Society.

To Davies Gilbert Esq, M.P. V.P.R.S. &c. &c.
Salzburgh, July 1, 1827

MY DEAR SIR

Yesterday, on my arrival here, I found your two letters. I am sorry I did not receive the one you were so good as to address to me at Ravenna; nor can I account for its miscarriage. I commissioned a friend there to transmit to me my letters from that place after my departure, and I received several, even so late as the middle of May, at Laybach, which had been sent to Italy, and afterwards to Illyria. I did not write to you again, because I always entertained hopes of being able to give a better account of the state of my health. I am sorry to say the expectations of my physicians of a complete and rapid recovery have not been realized. I have gained ground, under the most favourable circumstances, very slowly; and although I have had no new attack, and have regained, to a certain extent, the use of my limbs, yet the tendency of the system to accumulate blood in the head still continues, and I am obliged to counteract it by a most rigid vegetable diet, and by frequent bleedings with leeches and blisterings, which of course keep me very low. From my youth up to last year, I had suffered, more or less, from a slight hemorrhoidal affection; and the fullness of the vessels, then only a slight inconvenience, becomes a serious and dangerous evil in the head, to which it seems to have transferred. I am far from despairing of an ultimate recovery but it must be a work of time, and the vessels which have been over distended only slowly regain their dimensions and tone: and for my recovery, not only diet and regimen and physical discipline, but a freedom from anxiety, and from all business and all intellectual exertion, is absolutely required.

Under these circumstances, I feel it would be highly imprudent and perhaps fatal for me, to return, and to attempt to perform the official duties of the President of the Royal Society. And as I had not other feeling for that high and honourable situation, except the hope of feeling useful to society, so I would not keep it a moment without the security of being able to devote myself to the labour and attention it demands. I beg therefore you will be so good as to communicate my resignation to the Council and to the Society at their first meeting in November, after the long vacation; stating the circumstances of my severe and long continued illness, as the cause. At the same time, I beg you will express to them how truly grateful I feel for the high honour they have done me in placing me in the chair for so many successive years. Assure them that I shall always take the same interest in the progress of the grand objects of the Society, and throughout the whole of my life endeavour to contribute to their advancement, and to the prosperity of the body.

Should circumstances prevent me from sending, or you from receiving any other communication from me before the autumn (for nothing is more uncertain than the post in Austria, as they take time to read the letters), I hope this, which I shall go to Bavaria to send, will reach you safe, and will be sufficient to settle the affair of resignation.

It was my intention to have said nothing on the subject of my successor. I will support by all the means in my power the person that the leading members of the Society shall place in the chair; but I cannot resist an expression of satisfaction in the hope you held out, that an illustrious friend of the Society, illustrious from his talents, his former situation, and, I might say, his late conduct, is likely to be my successor.

I wish my name to be in the next Council, as I shall certainly return, Deo volente, before the end of the session, and I may, I think, be of use; and likewise, because I hope it may be clearly understood that my feelings for the Society are, as they always were, those of warm attachment and respect. Writing still makes my head ache, and raises my pulse. I will therefore conclude, my dear Sir, in returning you my sincere thanks for the trouble you have had on my account, and assuring you that I am

Your obliged and grateful friend and servant

H. DAVY.

Pray acknowledge the receipt of this letter, by addressing me, "poste restante, Laybach, Illyria, Austria;" and let me know if **MR HUDSON** *is still Assistant-Secretary, and where Mr South is. I sent this letter from Frauenstein, Bavaria, July 2, that it may not be opened, as all my letters were at Salzburgh. There was one of them must have amused Prince Metternich, on the state of parties in England, from a Member of the Upper House.*

As a consequence of this letter, the Council of the Royal Society, by a resolution passed at a very full meeting held on the 6th November 1827, appointed Mr Davies Gilbert to fill the chair. Sir Humphry Davy moved to Rome in early 1829 and died in Geneva a few months later, but not from haemorrhoidal affection!

From the archives of the Royal Society it is apparent that James was kept very busy with his duties in assistance to the many committees that had been formed in response to varied pressures. He catalogued the manuscripts and books held by the Library and attended on the various Fellows of the Royal Society at whatever time of the day or night they chose to visit the Library. The Library Committee was occasionally embroiled in differences of opinion with James as they were with future Librarians and there were often dramatic moments. One Librarian was even dismissed from his post for bringing a lady into his apartment! Not James, of course! James was compelled to ask the committee for extra pay to compensate him for the long hours he was expected to work.

Davies Gilbert in 1838, the second President of The Royal Society under whom James Hudson served. James named his eldest son Gilbert and the name has been passed down through the Hudson family ever since.
[National Portrait Gallery]

A meeting of the Royal Society taking place in Somerset House. The President, believed to be Davies Gilbert, is flanked by the Secretary and Assistant Secretary. [The Royal Society]

In between those long hours of work James had managed to father two daughters; Mary Ann and Catherine Louise plus three sons: Gilbert (named after Mr Davies Gilbert, the President of the Royal Society at the time of the baby's birth), James (named after his father, grand-father and great-grandfather), and my great-grandfather, Humphry Davy Hudson (named after Sir Humphry Davy, the President of the Royal Society at the time of James' appointment).

The children were all baptised at the Church of St Mary le Strand which stands in the centre of the Strand and next door to Somerset House. In the 1960s, during my years as a Metropolitan Police Cadet, I was posted to Bow Street Police Station. I often walked the beat around the Strand and Somerset House which in those days contained The General Registry of Births, Marriages and Deaths, now housed at Kew.

The font at the Church of St Mary le Strand in London, where my great-grandfather, Humphry Davy Hudson and his brothers and sisters, were all baptised. [Hudson Collection]

WILLIAM IV TAKES OVER FROM
BROTHER GEORGE IV, 1830

James and Mary Hudson's eldest daughter, Mary Ann, sadly died at the tender age of three years old. She had been staying with Mary's parents in Calow, Chesterfield, and was buried at Bakewell on 11th October 1831.

The family was back in mourning again just two months later when Ann Greaves' second husband, William, died at the Rutland Arms. He was buried a few days before Christmas on 23rd December 1831 in Bakewell churchyard in a grave very close to that of Ann's first husband, James Hudson. Ann again took over the licence of The Rutland and her son, Billy Greaves, became the postmaster. Billy also carried on farming several hundred acres of land at Haddon Hall Farm on the outskirts of Bakewell.

Silhouette of Mrs Ann Greaves by White Watson c1820-1830. [Derby Museums & Art Gallery]

No paintings of Ann Greaves are believed to exist, but a profile silhouette of her from around this time survives. It was drawn by White Watson, the mineralogist, geologist, marble worker, sculptor, antiquary and chronicler who lived in Bath House, Bakewell, and who died in 1835. Although Mrs Greaves is shown wearing a mob-cap in the silhouette her profile reminds me of several of my female relatives!

The Rutland Arms stables continued to provide horses for daily coaches to and from London, Manchester, Birmingham, Nottingham and Sheffield, the hotel providing refreshment and accommodation for the many travellers. The area around The Rutland and The Square was the hub of the local community.

Meanwhile, back in London during the months of April to July 1831 and January and February of 1832, James Hudson was engaged in hourly observations of the standard barometer, the water barometer and the mountain barometer *"with experimental investigations into the phenomena of its periodical oscillation"*.

He wrote *"I proposed to undertake as extensive a series of hourly observations on this instrument as my official duties and the state of my health would permit; to prosecute such experimental investigations into collateral branches of the inquiry, as the anomalies presenting themselves might require; and to institute, finally, a comparison between my own results and those derived from the labours of other observers, both in this country and on the Continent".*

He received assistance from his wife and recorded that *"through the assistance of Mrs HUDSON, who supplied my place as the observer for six hours of the night during these thirty days, and whose estimation in registering the instruments was found, on every comparison, to accord with my own"*.

Over three hundred documents have survived on record relating to experiments carried out in which James Hudson was involved during his time at the Royal Society.

By 1835, James and Mary Hudson and the children had moved from their apartment in Somerset House to a villa residence in Foxley Road, Kennington, a short carriage ride away from the Royal Society Headquarters. On 2nd April 1835, after a long and persistent period of illness, James resigned from the Royal Society. A few days later, Mary gave birth to another son, Charles. Not long after the birth of Charles, his mother, Mary Hudson, died.

In 1836, James applied for the post of Secretary of the New London or Metropolitan University, now known as The University of London. In order to support this application he collected fifty testimonials from prominent members of the Royal Society.

This *Private Impression of Testimonials* was published in 1838, printed by Bradbury and Evans of Whitefriars, Printers-Extraordinary to The Queen and inscribed *"with every sentiment of deep and grateful respect"*. Only four copies are to my knowledge still in existence, one in the archives of the University of London and the others in the possession of members of the family. The testimonials speak of the high regard held in James by Sir Humphry Davy, who had recommended him for the post of Assistant Secretary in the first place, and of Dr William Hyde Wollaston, Mr Davies Gilbert and HRH The Duke of Sussex, all Presidents of the Royal Society. They tell of James Hudson being highly qualified in Literature, Science, Modern Languages, Greek and Latin as well as his extensive travels abroad in the execution of his duties.

Prince Augustus Frederick, the Duke of Sussex in 1825. He was Queen Victoria's favourite uncle and gave her away at her wedding. He was the third President of The Royal Society under whom James Hudson served and one of the authors of a testimonial for his application for the post at the University of London. [National Portrait Gallery]

One of the testimonials from John George Children, a former Secretary of the Royal Society, who by 1837 was the Keeper of the British Museum, reads as follows:

British Museum
23rd January, 1837.

My Dear Sir,

I have been, like all the world, a good deal hors-de-combat by the prevalent Epidemic, and otherwise so much occupied, that I have been unable to write to you till now.

As I do not know the Nature of the Office which you are a Candidate for, I cannot at present judge of your qualifications to fill it:- but if it be one which requires Talent, Industry, and Integrity; a knowledge of Science and Modern Languages, and, I believe I may add, Greek and Latin; then I do not hesitate to say, that you are amply and admirably qualified to undertake it: and from the long series of years during which I have had the pleasure of knowing you, privately and officially, I am confident you will discharge its duties perfectly to the satisfaction of your superiors, and with credit to yourself; and very heartily I wish you may succeed in obtaining it!

I am ever,

My Dear Sir,

Faithfully yours,

JOHN GEO. CHILDREN
JAMES HUDSON, ESQ.

Sir John George Children in 1826, the renowned chemist, mineralogist and zoologist and author of the testimonial for James Hudson's application for the post at the University of London shown above.
[National Portrait Gallery]

The University of London has since confirmed that, in spite of his excellent collection of Testimonials, James was unsuccessful in his application for the post of Secretary of the New London University. However, printed on the frontispiece of the copy of his Testimonials currently held in the Library of the University of London, is the following dedication from James Hudson to his mother, Mrs Ann Greaves:

"To Mrs Greaves of Bakewell the Beloved Mother to whom I am indebted, Under the Blessing of a Gracious Providence, for every earthly happiness, and for all the worldly success attended on my humble exertions: I dedicate, with a willing and grateful heart, this Private and Confidential copy, of the Testimonies of Character, and collected body of evidence, of that successful result of her maternal care and never-failing exertions, which make me, if possible, in a still higher degree her grateful, dutiful, and affectionate Son, James Hudson."

Meanwhile, back in Bakewell, Billy Greaves had met Mary Burgoyne, the daughter of the head keeper of the Chatsworth Estate. Billy and Mary were married in Edensor Parish Church on 1st February 1837 in a double wedding with her twin sister, Catherine. One of the witnesses at their wedding was Joseph Paxton, the head gardener to the Sixth Duke of Devonshire at nearby Chatsworth House.

At the time of the wedding the village of Edensor would have seemed like a building site as Paxton, together with designer, John Robertson, were in the process of constructing a model village for the Duke in the area surrounding the church. The fourteenth century St Peter's church used for their wedding day would have been much smaller in 1837 and without its present day Sir George Gilbert Scott spire. The wedding guests would also have been able to observe signs of the building of Paxton's Great Conservatory growing in the gardens at nearby Chatsworth.

Joseph Paxton in May 1836, who was a witness at Billy Greaves first wedding and whose sister-in-law became Billy Greaves' second wife.
[Devonshire Collection, Chatsworth. Reproduced by permission of Chatsworth Settlement Trustees]

VICTORIA, THE LAST OF THE HANOVERIANS, SUCCEEDS HER UNCLE WILLIAM, 1837

Billy and Mary soon produced a daughter, Ann, named after his mother, Mrs Greaves, and she was baptised at Bakewell Church on 16th November 1837. Sadly, she only lived for 17 months and was buried in Bakewell Churchyard on 16th April 1839. The funeral must have been extremely distressing for all concerned as the death occurred when her mother, Mary Greaves, was only a few days away from giving birth to her second child.

A few days after the birth of little Ann Greaves, James Hudson remarried, this time to Maria Chubb at Cole Orton Parish Church in Leicestershire on 2nd December 1837. Maria was the 33 year-old daughter of an innkeeper from Leicestershire. One of the witnesses at the wedding was James' half-brother, Billy Greaves.

Whilst the whole country mourned the death on 20th June 1837 of King William IV extensive preparations were being made for the coronation of the young Queen Victoria on 28th June 1838.

On 13th May 1839, at the Rutland Arms, Mary Greaves gave birth to a son, who was, unimaginatively, named William! The birth took the life-blood out of Mary and she never fully recovered.

In London in 1839 James Hudson applied for and became the first Secretary of the recently formed Royal Agricultural Society of England (RASE). This post also required him to be the Editor of The Journal of the RASE. He negotiated his own very simple terms of employment and in a hand-written agreement dated 25th July 1839, which is still in existence (see over), he wrote:

> *"The Secretary & Editor in consideration of a salary of £400 a year is to provide a Clerk, who shall attend daily at the Rooms of the Society, and to devote his exclusive Attention to the Affairs of the Society. He is to attend all meetings of the Society & of the Committee, to be ready to give his assistance when required to the Sub Committees and to prepare the Journal for Publication subject to the Directions of the Journal Committee. James Hudson 5 Cavendish Square July 25. 1839."*

He then signed and dated the agreement. The committee of the RASE would regret in years to come the loose definition of James' duties and responsibilities as laid down in the agreement.

The Secretary & Editor in consideration of a Salary of £400 a year is to provide a Clerk, who shall attend daily at the Rooms of the Society, & to devote his exclusive Attention to the Affairs of the Society. He is to attend all meetings of the Society & of the Committee to be ready to give his Assistance when required to the Sub Committees & to prepare the Journal for Publication subject to the Directions of the Journal Committee.

James Hudson.

5 Cavendish Square
July 25. 1839.

A copy of the original agreement of the duties of the new post of Secretary of The Royal Agricultural Society of England and Editor of its Journal handwritten by James Hudson on 25th July 1839. [The Royal Agricultural Society of England]

Back in Derbyshire, Mary Greaves, nee Burgoyne, weakened by the recent birth of her son, William, died of consumption at her parent's home at Edensor at the young age of 26 years. Her twin sister, Catherine, was at her side when she died. She was buried at Edensor Church on 19th January 1840.

In London on 26th October 1840, James Hudson's new wife, Maria, gave birth to a daughter, Sophia, who was later baptised at St Mark's Church, Kennington. James must have felt that by then he had reached a certain position in society when an entry in the 'Nobility &c.' section of *Pigot's Surrey Directory 1840* lists him as *"James Hudson, esq. 7 Foxley Road, Brixton"*.

Although in 1840 the Kennington Oval, only a few streets away from Foxley Road, was still a market garden, I am sure James would have been a regular spectator at the Oval a few years later in 1845 when it had been turned into the famous headquarters of Surrey Cricket Club. Cricket has been a great love of many members of the Hudson family throughout the generations as will be seen later.

James & Maria Hudson, their children and servants continued to live in Kennington but it was not long before they moved into accommodation in the RASE Headquarters, firstly at 5 Cavendish Square, Westminster, and later when the RASE relocated to 12 Hanover Square, just a few hundred yards away. They had two more children, Maria in 1844 and John George in 1847, who were both baptised at St George's Church, Hanover Square, Westminster. In the late 1960s, as a young Police Constable, I worked at West End Central Police Station in Saville Row and lived for several years in a Police Section House in Soho. During that period I regularly worshipped at the above St George's Church in Hanover Square. If only I had been aware of our family's history then!

In 1842 the distinguished Victorian artist and member of the Royal Academy, Richard D Ansdell, painted a picture of the officers and members of the Royal Agricultural Society of England at their Country Meeting at Clifton Downs, Bristol. He first painted an individual portrait of each of the 150 persons before transferring all 150 onto the 30 feet x 8 feet canvas. The original painting now hangs in the committee room of the headquarters of the RASE at the Royal Showground in Stoneleigh, Warwickshire and is extremely impressive. The individual portrait of James Hudson shows him at the age of 38 years in morning dress, high collar, top hat, pointed nose, long sideburns with kiss curls. There have been many Hudson family members with pointed noses, but not to my knowledge that many with kiss curls!

Portrait of James Hudson at the Royal Agricultural Society of England Country Meeting at Clifton Downs, Bristol, painted in 1842 by Richard D Ansdell RA. [The Royal Agricultural Society of England]

In his official position as Secretary of the RASE and unofficially as a native of Bakewell, James Hudson regularly visited the annual Bakewell Agricultural Show. The early shows were held on land surrounding his birthplace, the Rutland Arms Inn.

In 1843, during a visit to Chatsworth, Queen Victoria was driven through the middle of Bakewell in an open carriage to the cheers of the assembled townsfolk. The town was decorated with flags, garlands, ribbons, flowers and a large flag was hoisted on Castle Hill. She was also driven in a carriage through Paxton's Great Conservatory at Chatsworth. The giant glasshouse had been brightly illuminated for the occasion by 12,000 lamps attached to the ribs.

Billy Greaves' first wife, Mary, had been the daughter of the head keeper on the Chatsworth Estate and for his second wife he took another Mary, this time Mary Bown, aged 48 and the elder sister of Sarah, the wife of Joseph Paxton. Mary was also employed on the Chatsworth Estate and had been living at Beeley. Billy and Mary Bown were married at St Anne's Church, Beeley, on 6th April 1844.

The story of the whirlwind romance with and marriage to Joseph Paxton of Mary Greaves' sister, Sarah Bown, is worth recounting. Most of the tale can be found in the *Handbook to Chatsworth and Hardwick* written by William Spencer Cavendish, the Bachelor Duke of Devonshire in 1844. He related that on 9th May 1826 Paxton, aged only 22 years, arrived at Chatsworth very early in the morning for his first day's work and, having looked around the gardens and setting the men to work, he went to the kitchens where he met Hannah Gregory, the Duke's housekeeper, and her niece, Sarah Bown. Joseph and Sarah apparently fell in love at first sight and were married at Edensor Church a few months later. Sarah came from a wealthy Matlock family and had a dowry of £5,000, whereas Paxton's starting salary as Head Gardener at Chatsworth was just £65 per annum. What a catch!

Sarah Bown c.1827 at Chatsworth House shortly before she married Joseph Paxton.
[Devonshire Collection, Chatsworth. Reproduced by permission of Chatsworth Settlement Trustees]

William Spencer, the Sixth Duke of Devonshire, who worked very closely with Joseph and Sarah Paxton on the improvements at Chatsworth. [National Portrait Gallery]

Paxton, affectionately known as 'Dob', soon became Head Forester as well as Head Gardener and was indispensable to the Duke. He was given the task of re-designing the gardens at Chatsworth and building the model village at Edensor. In gratitude to Paxton the Duke built a magnificent Italian-style villa called Barbrook for Joseph and Sarah to live in the park. Soon Paxton was acting as the Duke's agent, not only for Chatsworth but also for several of the Duke's other estates. These extra duties continually took Paxton away from Chatsworth and from Sarah!

Sarah and her children spent a lonely existence at Barbrook whilst Joseph travelled the world. She helped to run the estate in his absence whilst he gained commissions to build private gardens and houses all over the country. Paxton's greatest commission was the design of the famous Crystal Palace in Hyde Park for the Great Exhibition of 1851. This he modelled on his Great Conservatory at Chatsworth. Queen Victoria rewarded him with a knighthood. Paxton later became a Member of Parliament and a director of the Midland Railway Co.. He was seldom at Barbrook!

Sarah Paxton was a formidable woman. Several years older than Paxton, she also towered over him in height. George Chadwick credits Sarah as second only to the Duke of Devonshire in enabling Paxton's career. He records:

"It was Sarah's ability to judge a situation coolly (especially a financial one) and to act responsibly that was to be the greatest help to her husband. It was Sarah who sat at home at Barbrook or in the estate office nearby attending to the day-to-day routine of Chatsworth life for Paxton, whilst he was ranging up and down the country or the Continent on his many interests. It was Sarah who in a very real sense managed his affairs at the Derbyshire end whilst Paxton operated his parliamentary career, business interests and professional practice in London. Nor was Sarah a passive partner in their enterprises: although Paxton was very much the head of the concern the initiative on many things came from his wife and her approbation was always something to be sought by him. A growing family – eight children, five daughters and one son of which survived – constant attendance on estate and house duties at Chatsworth, and playing 'anchor man' in Paxton's business and professional team: this was no small feat, even for the able and intelligent woman that Paxton met on his first morning at Chatsworth and married six months later."

Mrs Hannah Gregory c1827 who was Sarah Paxton's aunt and the housekeeper to the Dukes of Devonshire for 50 years. [Devonshire Collection, Chatsworth. Reproduced by permission of Chatsworth Settlement Trustees]

Let me make a couple more connections with the Hudson/Greaves family. The mother of sisters Sarah and Mary Bown, who on marriage became Lady Paxton and the second Mrs Billy Greaves respectively, was a lady from Matlock whose maiden name was Sarah Gregory. Her sister, Hannah Gregory – the aunt of Sarah and Mary Bown – was the housekeeper to the Dukes of Devonshire for 50 years. Hannah began working at Chatsworth under the 5th Duke, and when the 6th Duke inherited Chatsworth in 1811, she continued to serve him faithfully until her death on 4th October 1843. Mary Bown, before she became Mrs Billy Greaves, and one of Hannah Gregory's nieces mentioned above, was by her aunt's side when she died, aged 77 years, in the Stag Parlour, her bedroom in Chatsworth House for many years.

Another relative by marriage was George Stephenson 'the father of the railways' who invented *The Rocket*, the first 'modern' locomotive. He lived nearby at Tapton House just outside Chesterfield. On 11th April 1848 George married his housekeeper, Miss Ellen Gregory, only four months before he died on 12th August in the same year. Ellen was his third wife. She was a daughter of Richard Gregory of Meadow Place Farm, Conksbury, just above Lathkill Dale, near Bakewell. Richard and his daughter, Ellen, were related to Sarah Gregory, Paxton's mother-in-law, and Hannah Gregory, the Duke of Devonshire's housekeeper.

George Stephenson in the 1840s who married distant relative Ellen Gregory just four months before he died. [Science and Society Picture Library]

George Stephenson and Joseph Paxton were both shareholders of the Manchester, Buxton, Matlock and Midland Junction Railway. Stephenson also owned a small farm in Derbyshire where he experimented with stockbreeding, new types of manure and animal food. He also developed a method of fattening chickens in half the usual time. This he did by shutting them in dark boxes after a heavy feed!

In 1841 George Stephenson held the position of President of the North Derbyshire Agricultural Society, the organisers of the annual Bakewell Show. Fifteen years later, in 1856, Sir Joseph Paxton held the same post.

In a speech at the 1844 Bakewell Show Dinner held at The Rutland, Billy Greaves, who was also an experienced farmer, said he had discovered a great advantage in sowing a herb called comfrey. It was hardy, gave three crops a year, cattle were fond of it and it produced great quantities of milk without injuring the flavour. In 1985, over 140 years later, farmers were being told in the British press about experimental work on the possibilities of using comfrey! What foresight!

In 1845 Billy, Mary and their young son, William Greaves, moved from The Rutland Arms to Matlock Bath where Billy became the proprietor of the Old Bath Royal Hotel and Posting House. The Old Bath had been the first hotel to be built in Matlock Bath and stood overlooking the River Derwent in what is now the enormous public car park beside Holy Trinity Church. The stables were on the site of today's Fishpond Hotel. An old journal explains that:

"The principal one [hotel] is denominated the Old Bath, and it is a spacious building capable of affording accommodations to nearly one hundred visitors. At this inn there is an excellent assembly room, lighted with elegant glass chandeliers; and a hot and cold bath are included within the establishment. All the warm springs issue from between fifteen and thirty yards above the level of the river: the temperature is 68 degrees of Fahrenheit's thermometer. There are two good baths, one for the ladies and another for the gentlemen and also hot and shower baths of any temperature required.

Note: The general terms for accommodation are as follows. A bed-chamber is five shillings per week; a private parlour from fourteen shillings to a guinea. Breakfast, one shilling and threepence; dinner at the public table, two shillings; tea, optional, but when taken, one shilling; supper, one shilling and sixpence. Bathing, sixpence each time."

An old postcard of Holy Trinity Church, the Old Bath Hotel and Pavilion, Matlock Bath. The site of the hotel in the centre is now a car park but the Royal Petrifying Well can still be seen against the back wall. [Peter Aspey Collection]

The hotel was rebuilt in the late 1800s and accidentally burnt down in 1927. The brickwork showing the outline of several of the outbuildings and stables of the hotel can still be faintly traced in the wall at the rear of the car park next to the church. Also to be seen in the car park is a tufa grotto surrounding the original warm springs that still flow out of the hillside. They once formed the famous bath that the Romans had discovered so long ago. This bath was named the Royal Petrifying Well in honour of Princess Victoria's visit to the hotel in 1832.

Billy employed 28 labourers, post boys and grooms at the Old Bath Hotel. Meanwhile, he continued to farm the 800 acres of Haddon Farm just like his father, William Greaves, and the late James Hudson had before him. Haddon Hall had been closed down and mothballed by the first Duke of Rutland in 1702 when he and his family made Belvoir Castle, in Leicestershire, their principal seat.

Haddon Hall remained closed until 1912, the year in which my Dad was born, when the ninth Duke decided to renovate the building. This must have been an exciting project as Haddon had not been the victim of any distasteful Georgian or Victorian restoration. It had only been opened for occasional visits by prominent guests, including Princess Victoria during the Royal visit to Derbyshire in 1832 mentioned above. Also in 1836 a ball was held at the Hall by the Duke to celebrate his son, the Marquis of Granby's 21st birthday and all the tenantry of the estate were invited.

Meanwhile, whilst Billy and his family were ensconced in Matlock Bath, Ann Greaves continued to run The Rutland Arms. For the first time since 1809 the Post Office in Bakewell was moved away from the Inn and a new postmaster set up his office in the building opposite The Rutland by the old stables and now occupied by a chemist's shop.

The good old days of the monopoly of stagecoaches on the roads of England was coming to an end and the 'golden age' of the steam railway was just around the corner. George Stephenson, as explained earlier, was a distant relative of the Hudson family by marriage and had discovered a draper's assistant from near York called George Hudson. This gentleman was definitely not a relative! George Hudson, who later became known as 'The Railway King', had been very successful in identifying possible routes for future railway lines and at negotiating lucrative contracts with the various landowners. He became one of England's first business tycoons.

In 1849 The Manchester, Buxton, Matlock and Midland Junction Railway opened its line from Ambergate to Rowsley. George Stephenson, George Hudson, Joseph Paxton, and my great-great-grandfather, James Hudson from the Royal Agricultural Society, were all shareholders of the company. Paxton also designed the impressive station buildings at Matlock Bath and Rowsley on the line.

Paxton's original railway station building at Rowsley still survives as the focal point of the Peak Village shopping outlet.

Joseph Paxton's original Rowsley Station building is now the centrepiece of the Peak Village shopping outlet. [Hudson Collection]

The *Derby Mercury* of 6th June 1849 stated that *"The opening of this line took place on Monday, and the trains during the day (six each way), were well filled with passengers, chiefly on pleasure excursions. At Rowsley the scene on the arrival of each train was animated in the extreme, and very many of the pleasure seekers availed themselves of the gay looking and really costly vehicles placed at their disposal by Mr Greaves, of the Old Bath Royal Hotel, Matlock, and the Rutland Arms, Bakewell, as well as other conveyances, and made trips to the princely mansion of Chatsworth, or the venerable pile of grey old Haddon"*.

In 1851 Ann Greaves, at the sprightly old age of 73, was still the innkeeper of the Rutland Arms. She was ably assisted by a large staff together with three grand children, her grand-daughter Emily Bradley, who was the daughter of Ann (Hudson) Bradley, and grand-sons Alex Balmannie, the son of Ann's sister Mary (Hudson) Balmannie from the USA, and Charles Hudson, one of James' sons from London.

In those days, a horse-drawn carriage from The Rutland would have met every train on its arrival at Rowsley Station. By 1860 there would have only been a few toll roads still in existence and travel by coach would have become more of a

tourist attraction than an essential means of transport. However, each summer until 1895 a stagecoach ran three days a week from Sheffield to Buxton via Bakewell. It was rather similar to the current popularity of preserved steam trains.

On 1st May 1851 the Great Exhibition was opened by Queen Victoria inside the magnificent Crystal Palace built by Joseph Paxton in London's Hyde Park. Just imagine the excitement of Ann and the rest of my ancestors who were alive at that time journeying up to London, either by train or stagecoach, in order to visit this great event. I wonder if they stayed with James Hudson in Hanover Square?

Ann Greaves carried on running The Rutland until 1857, when at the grand old age of 80 she took her well-deserved retirement and moved to the Kirkmanshulme district of Manchester to be closer to her younger daughter, Ann Bradley, who lived there.

Joseph Paxton's revolutionary Crystal Palace standing in Hyde Park, London. The Palace was 1,848 feet long, 408 feet wide and 108 feet high. It required 4,500 tons of iron, 60,000 cubic feet of timber and needed over 293,000 panes of glass. It took 2,000 men just eight months to build.

This is believed to be the only known photograph of Mrs Ann Greaves. [Hudson Collection]

Ann Greaves' retirement coincided with Billy and Mary Greaves' return to Bakewell from Matlock Bath's Old Bath Royal Hotel. At long last, at the age of 50, Billy finally became the licensee of the Rutland Arms. Their return to Bakewell was marred just a few months later by the tragic death at sea of Billy's only son, William, aged 19 years. Billy had now lost both of his children.

The Rutland Arms continued to be the busy hub of the town. The 1857 edition of White's Directory of Derbyshire listed the following transport schedule for Bakewell:

From the Rutland Arms.

The undermentioned Coaches run only during the Summer season, excepting the two mails.
To Buxton; the Enterprise, at 6.0 p.m.
To Buxton; the Mail, at 11.30 a.m.
To Buxton; the Peak Guide, at 5.30 p.m.
To Manchester; the Mail, at 12.20 p.m.
To Manchester; the Union, at 10.20 a.m.
To Matlock; the Union, at 5.0 p.m.
To Rowsley Station; Omnibus from the Rutland Hotel, meets every train to & from, leaving Bakewell 30 minutes before the published time of the trains.
To Rowsley Station; the Mail, at 5.30 p.m.
To Rowsley Station; the Peak Guide, at 3.30 p.m.
To Sheffield; the Enterprise, daily at 10.0 a.m.
To Sheffield; the Mail, at 3.45 p.m.

My great-great-grandfather, James Hudson, posed for this portrait at a studio in Regent Street, London.
[Hudson Collection]

Another tragedy was soon to befall the family of Ann Greaves. As I mentioned earlier, the committee of the Royal Agricultural Society of England would, in years to come, regret the loose definition of James Hudson's duties and responsibilities of his post laid down in the agreement which he himself had drawn up. James had been Secretary of the RASE and Editor of their Journal for nearly 20 years when, on 27th May 1859, the Special Council discovered that an amount of money that James had collected from the three Country Meetings held at Salisbury, Chester and Warwick had not been paid into the Society's bank account. James was subsequently suspended from his post whilst an enquiry took place.

During this period of suspension James travelled up to Manchester to visit his mother, Ann Greaves. He went to stay with his sister, Ann Bradley, in Chorlton upon Medlock. Sadly, on 28th June 1859, James Hudson died in a house just a few streets away from the home of his retired mother. He had died of a diseased liver.

On 8th September 1859 *"Letters of Administration of the Personal estate and effects of James Hudson late of 12 Hanover square in the county of Middlesex Secretary of the Royal Agricultural Society of England deceased who died 28 June 1859 at 1 Norton terrace Stockport road near Manchester in the County of Lancaster were granted at the Principal Registry to Maria Hudson of Ashby-de-la-Zouch in the County of Leicester Widow the Relict of the said Deceased she having been first sworn."*

The Royal Agricultural Society of England later discovered that, some days before his death, James had executed a deed of assignment making over the whole of his effects for the benefit of his creditors. This more or less covered the shortfall. At the next meeting of the Special Council of the RASE it agreed *"to allow a deduction of 5% from the dividends for the purpose of helping the three youngest children and if sufficient to extend the same to the widow".* So James' widow, Maria, and their three youngest children were provided for until they were old enough to enter professions.

Back in Bakewell, Billy Greaves had become closely involved in the public life of the market town. In 1857 he was listed as a churchwarden at All Saint's Church. As well as farming locally from 1860-1865 he was the Secretary of the North Derbyshire Agricultural Society, the body that organised Bakewell Show each year. The Rutland Arms had been closely involved with the Show for many years. The meetings of the Show Committee and the regularly oversubscribed Agricultural Society annual dinners had always been held at the hotel.

Billy was also the Secretary of the High Peak Hunt which ritually took its stirrup cup in Rutland Square outside the hotel. He was a very tall, bulky and larger than life character and hunt followers often felt sorry for his horse as he clambered into the saddle! Nevertheless, he was an excellent rider.

On 11th March 1863 a meeting of townsfolk passed a resolution to adopt the formation of a Local Board to take over many of the civic matters which for so long were dealt with at the Vestry Meetings. Billy Greaves was one of only eight members of the great and the good of Bakewell invited to sit on that original board.

All of James & Mary Hudson's children in London had been educated at home by their Governess, Emma Cowdall, apart from young Mary Ann who died aged three. Gilbert was a clerk in the Coast Guard Headquarters in Custom House, London, later to become a Civil Servant at The Admiralty; James trained as a Shipwright's Apprentice in Woolwich dockyard and became a Shipwright before he retired to live in Guernsey; my great-grandfather, Humphry Davy Hudson, must have been impressed by tales he had heard of The Charge of the Light Brigade because in 1855 he joined the 11th (Prince Albert's Own) Regiment of (Light) Dragoons (Hussars), one of the famous regiments which, only a few months earlier, had been at the heart of the battle; Catherine Louisa worked as a Governess in Bath.

Humphry Davy, known to his colleagues as 'Davy' had joined up at the age of 23 and was in army barracks in Folkestone, Kent, waiting for the bulk of the 11th Hussars to return from the Crimea. Davy was promoted to Sergeant in 1858 and the regiment was based in Folkestone until 1861 when it was deployed to Ireland. For the next four years Davy was stationed at Island Bridge Barracks in Phoenix Park, Dublin. During his posting to Ireland, Davy married Harriet who was from Hythe in Kent, and whilst in Dublin she gave birth to a daughter, Annie, and a son, William, who was known as 'Will' and was my grandad. I am certain that Davy would have grabbed a spot of leave from the Army to take young Will to Manchester to visit his great-grandmother, Ann Greaves, whilst she was still alive!

On 17th April 1865 Humphry Davy bought himself out of the Army and joined the mounted branch of the Folkestone division of the Coast Guard. Whilst living in Folkestone Harriet had given birth to two more daughters, Mary Louisa and Emily Bradley Hudson, the latter named after Emily Bradley, who was Davy's aunt.

(Humphry) Davy Hudson in Folkestone in 1865 just after he had bought himself out of the 11th (Prince Albert's Own) Regiment of (Light) Dragoons (Hussars). [Hudson Collection]

THE DEATH OF ANN GREAVES

In 1866 the long, busy and dedicated life of the woman who had, together with her two husbands and for many years on her own run The Rutland Arms in Bakewell eventually came to an end. She had kept The Rutland for a total of 54 years. She had been the instigator of the famous Bakewell Pudding and a pillar of Bakewell society. On 11th July at the age of 88 years Ann Greaves died of old age. On 14th July the *Manchester Guardian* regretted that *"on the 11th inst in her 89th year at Levenshulme, Manchester, Ann Greaves, late of the Rutland Arms Hotel, Bakewell, had died"*. Her body was interred at St John's Church, in Longsight, Manchester.

Meanwhile, life went on without her and in April 1869 the Mounted Coastguard Service was abolished and Davy Hudson had to look for employment elsewhere. He decided to take his family northwards from Kent to the land of his father's birth – Derbyshire.

On 15th February 1870 he joined the Derbyshire Constabulary. In his police records, Davy is described as being 5'8½" tall, the same height as my father, Gill, and ½" taller than I had been when I joined the Metropolitan Police Force 96 years later.

(Humphry) Davy Hudson posing at a studio in London in 1869. [Hudson Collection]

Davy's children and his postings around the police stations of Derbyshire came thick and fast! In March 1870 whilst Davy was stationed in Derby, Harriet gave birth to another son, Humphry Davy, who was later to be nicknamed 'Daff'. After a posting to Higher Buxton Police Station in 1871 Davy was moved to Chapel-en-le-Frith where in 1872 they had their third daughter, Sophia Jane. The Derbyshire Constabulary certainly kept their officers on the move because by the birth of their third son, Gilbert James, in 1874, Davy and family were living in New Mills. It was now time for Davy to leave the force and to start looking around for a more stationary job! On his resignation from the Constabulary he failed to surrender his truncheon and handcuffs. These are now proudly displayed on the wall in the house of one of Davy's great-grandchildren in Bakewell.

At the beginning of 1874 Billy Greaves' second wife, Mary (née Bown), died of bronchitis aged 77. During her period of illness Billy had been offered much comfort and, as will be seen later, more than just a little sympathy from one of his young under-barmaids, Ellen Allsopp! Two years later in 1876, when Billy had reached the age of 69, he promoted Ellen to the position of third wife and they were duly married in Bakewell Church.

There are no photographs available of Billy Greaves. However, in 1888 as a token of their respect for him, several of his friends from the Bakewell area commissioned a full-length portrait of Billy painted by Mr Boadel of Liverpool. It would be fascinating to set eyes on this portrait!

Meanwhile, (Humphry) Davy had been searching for a less nomadic existence and on 16th April 1875, after excellent references from his uncle, Billy Greaves, he became the proprietor of the Castle and Commercial Hotel in Bakewell (now known as the Castle Hotel). Their arrival in Bakewell did not curtail the size of their family and Charles Greaves Hudson was duly born later the same year; Harriet (nick-named 'Queenie') arrived in 1876; and finally Ellen (known as 'Nell') was born in 1879. They were all born at the Castle Hotel. My great-grandfather's family of ten children was now complete.

Young Will Hudson a few years before he left home aged 16 to work in Derby.
[Hudson Collection]

The Castle Hotel was famous for its regular horse fairs held in the street in front of the hotel since the early 1800s. Before 1810 the fairs had been held on open land alongside Coombs Road on the other side of Bakewell Bridge. This land later became formal gardens for the Castle and Commercial Hotel before being divided into allotments where, in more recent years, my green-fingered cousin, John Hudson, grew the most wonderful dahlias. That same piece of land has now been turned into a flourishing car park owned by one of Will Hudson's great-grandchildren.

My Grandad, Will, began work as a 16 year-old apprentice ironmonger in Bakewell. He later moved to Derby where he learned his trade with an iron-founder, George H Handley.

In the meantime, Davy became Bakewell's delegate to the Derbyshire Licensed Victuallers' Association. He was an active member of the Dorothy Vernon Masonic Lodge which, until the new Town Hall was built in 1890, held their lodge meetings in the Rutland Arms. He was also involved with the Oddfellows, was a keen member of the Conservative party and on 7th January 1880 he was appointed to fill a vacancy on the Bakewell Local Board. In 1885 Davy was elected at the head of the poll with 266 votes and pushed the popular Archdeacon Balston, who was formerly the Headmaster of Eton, into second place. He remained on the Local Board until the time of his death.

The *Buxton Advertiser* of 11th April 1885 reported that:

> *"The result of the Bakewell Board election, made known on Wednesday afternoon, is that the three old members have been re-elected. Mr H D Hudson is first on the list, having beaten the Ven. Archdeacon Balston by a solitary vote. Our poet thus sings of*

DAVID'S VICTORY
Our Humphry Davy bears a name
Inscribed on History's roll of fame;
A son of Mars and valiant soul,
He bravely fought, and heads the poll,
Keen was the fight and stern the foe,
Ere Humphry dealt the fatal blow,
He reared his standards in the fight,
And put the valiant Knocks to flight.
His banner bore the strange device-
"Beer, Church The State and - all that's nice"
Not beer alone – the battle won-
Our David is an amorous one-
And Mother Bakewell's favourite son-

The victor, in honour of his victory, will deliver the following address at the next meeting of the Bakewell Local Board:-

To the Chairman:

In most things I agree with you.
My politics are jingo blue;
But yet to progress I'm inclined,
And for improvements have a mind,
I think sir, 'tis a dire disgrace,
And tell you plainly to your face,
The Town Hall is a wretched place.
'Tis not perhaps your fault, I own,
In public spirit I'm alone.

But let us from our slumbers rise,
And wipe the dust from Tory eyes.
I think if Rads could rule the town,
This wretched fossil would come down,
And from its ashes would arise,
A structure that the town would prize."

Perhaps the town was listening to Humphry Davy because four years later, in 1889, the corner stone for the new and current Town Hall was laid!

On 5th February 1887 in Derby, Will married his first wife, Sarah Elizabeth Hannah Sisson, the daughter of a Derby licensed victualler. It would appear that Will must have been influenced by his father, Humphry Davy's close connection with the Derbyshire Licensed Victuallers Association for his choice of bride! Just nine months later they had a daughter, Ethel, who later married Bill Eyre, a member of a family of building contractors and funeral directors in Great Longstone.

My great-grandfather, (Humphry) Davy Hudson posed for this signed photograph in Derby in November 1888 just eight months before he died. [Hudson Collection]

On Tuesday 30th July 1889 Humphry Davy went to Derby to watch the Derbyshire v Surrey cricket match at the County Ground with Will. This was a memorable match because the Surrey players were unhappy with the Derbyshire selectors for including the Australian demon fast bowler, Frederick Robert Spofforth, in their team. Spofforth had recently married a girl from Derbyshire and had decided to settle in the town. It was generally expected that one had to live in the area for two years before representing the county but the Derbyshire Committee had quickly amended their rules to allow him to be included in the team that day. Surrey decreed that they would only honour the fixture if the home side was described on all literature to do with the match as *"Derbyshire, plus Mr Spofforth"*!

Fred Spofforth first came to prominence in 1878 when he bowled W.G. Grace for a duck at Lords in a match between the MCC and the Australian touring side. The next year Spofforth became the first bowler ever to take a hat-trick in a test match when he performed the feat at Sydney against the English tourists

Humphry Davy's love of cricket has been passed down to the rest of the family and since those days many members of several generations of the Hudson family, including myself, have played for Bakewell Cricket Club.

After an enjoyable day at the County Ground they went back to Will's house in Derby and at the end of an evening of socialising with his son and several of his old friends from the Derby Police, including Superintendent Jepson, Humphry Davy decided to call it a day and at around midnight he went to his bedroom. Will later heard a loud sound in his father's room and hurried in to find his father had collapsed on the floor. Humphry Davy never recovered and within ten minutes he had died.

His funeral was held at the Cemetery in Bakewell three days later. *The High Peak News* reported that:

Fred 'The Demon' Spofforth, the Australian fast bowler, who starred for Derbyshire against Surrey in the cricket match in Derby that Davy Hudson had been watching on the day he died).
[Hulton Archive/Getty Images)]

"The funeral of Mr Humphry Davy Hudson, of the Castle Hotel, took place on Friday, at the Cemetery. Not only was the greatest respect possible shown to the deceased's memory, but in most of the shops in the town business was entirely suspended during the afternoon. Along the route taken from the Castle Hotel to the Cemetery there was not a single window to be seen that had not either its blind drawn, or was shuttered. In the memory of the oldest inhabitant, there has not a more solemn and imposing cortege followed a resident of Bakewell to his last resting place. A start was made from the Castle Hotel at two o'clock, and following immediately after the hearse was a carriage occupied by the deceased's four sons, William, Humphry Davy, Gill and Charley; next came Mr. H. Watson (son-in-law) and Mr. W. Townley (cousin), and Mr. W. Greaves, of the Rutland Arms Hotel (uncle of the deceased), in his own carriage."

The first attempt at a moustache by Will Hudson seen here in this photograph taken in Derby. He was aged about 27 years. He sported a moustache for the rest of his life! [Hudson Collection]

Humphry Davy's old cricketing friend and former police colleague, Superintendent Jepson, was one of the bearers at the funeral.

Humphry Davy's widow, Harriet, took over the licence of the Castle Hotel and ran it for several years with the assistance of three of her daughters Mary, Emily and Sophia.

On 8th May 1892 Will Hudson's wife, Sarah, died of acute pneumonia at their house in Peartree Avenue, Derby, where they had lived next door to Sarah's mother. Will stayed in Derby with his daughter, Ethel, for a few more months, but in 1894 he returned to Bakewell and took over the licence of the Castle & Commercial Hotel from his mother. Will was to be the licensee at The Castle for the next 23 years. His mother, Harriet, and her five unmarried sons and daughters moved to the Fairfield district of Buxton.

Will Hudson's return to Bakewell coincided with the death of his great uncle, Billy Greaves, who died at the Rutland Arms Hotel on 13th February 1894 at the age of 86 years after a short illness. The *Derby Mercury* of 21st February regretted that:

"Mr William Greaves, proprietor of the Rutland Arms Hotel, Bakewell, died at his residence on Wednesday morning. He had reached the 87th year of his age, but until the last few weeks he was able to get about. Deceased, who was widely known and highly respected, kept the Rutland Arms Hotel for about a quarter of a century. The family formerly resided at Matlock Bath, where they kept a large establishment, and from that place Mr Greaves removed to Bakewell. Mr Greaves was the son of William and Ann Greaves, who kept the hotel before him, and was born in 1807, in the same house as that in which he has lived and died, and was consequently 86 years of age. His father died in 1831, after which he, with his mother jointly, carried on the hotel business until 1866, when his mother also died. Up to the time of the railway to Manchester being opened from Rowsley, which was about 1862, the deceased was largely interested in a company of coach proprietors, running between London and Manchester. Four or five coaches per day regularly pulled up at the doors of the Rutland, and he was responsible for 'horsing' them a part of the journey. From fifty to sixty horses were regularly kept for this purpose. Old inhabitants will speak with a glow of pride of the time when Her Majesty's mail drove through the town every

morning, and of the old 'Peverill' and 'The Bruce' which used to run between Derby and Manchester, and even the names of John Sturby and 'Old Burdett', two celebrated drivers, are now called to mind. Mr Greaves was married three times. His first wife was Miss Burgoyne, daughter of the head keeper on the Chatsworth estate. By her he had two children, a son and a daughter. The latter died in infancy, and the former in 1858. His second wife was a Miss Bown, a sister to Lady Paxton, and by her there was no issue. After her death, now many years ago, he again married, Miss Allsopp, a daughter of Mr Allsopp, of Hucknall-Torkard, who now survives him. In addition to the hotel business Mr Greaves was one of the largest farmers in Derbyshire. Haddon Hall farm, which he held under the Duke of Rutland for the greater portion of his life, is something over 800 acres in extent. He was one of the earliest members of the Royal Agricultural Society, and has acted as a judge in connection with the shows of that society.

Only two or three years ago the committee paid him the high compliment of electing him a 'life Fellow' of that distinguished society. He was also one of the first founders of the Bakewell Farmers' Club, and was also elected on its committee. He became a member of the Bakewell Local Board soon after its formation, and was also a member for some years of the Bakewell Board of Guardians. These were, however, uncongenial spheres for his energies, and he retired from them some 20 years ago. About five or six years ago his many friends in Bakewell and neighbourhood presented him, as a token of respect, with a full-length portrait of himself painted in oil, by Mr Boadel, of Liverpool. Mr Greaves was a keen sportsman. There were few in the High Peak Hunt who were his equals at a high gate or a stone wall, whilst he was equally at home as a 'whip' on a four-in-hand coach, one of which he once drove from Bakewell to London. As a citizen, he was a liberal supporter to all public charities, schools, &c. The poor of Bakewell have lost in him a kind and benevolent friend. The chief mourners were Mr. W. A. Greaves, son of the deceased; Mr Wilkinson, Mr James & Wm. Hudson. Several gentlemen from the town and district followed in carriages. After these came the employees of the deceased. The tradesmen of the town followed."

Whilst I had been aware that both of Billy's children by his first wife, Mary (Burgoyne), Mary and William Greaves, had predeceased him, it was only when I tracked down the above newspaper cutting that I realised that Billy had fathered another son, shown in the funeral report as Mr W A Greaves, one of the chief mourners. A little detective work revealed that Billy's surviving son, William Henry Allsop, was born on 26th April 1873 in Nether Hallam, Sheffield, and that the mother, Miss Ellen Allsop, had been Billy's under-barmaid at the Rutland Arms. She only became his wife in 1876 after the death of Mary Greaves in 1874. However, the baby was born three years earlier at the house of Ellen's brother, Henry Allsop.

Young William probably spent his early years in Sheffield where he could be kept out of the limelight. At the time of baby William's birth, Billy's second wife, Mary (Bown) had been very much alive!

In 1891 Billy's son, William, is shown on the Census for The Rutland Arms as his 'nephew', William H Allsop, and Billy employed him on his farm. By 1894 at Billy's funeral he was using the surname Greaves, and by 1899, on the day of his wedding to Mabel Edith Palmer, his full name was William Henry Allsop Greaves. He was described as a 'Gentleman' of Great Longstone. Young William married a girl from his mother's Nottinghamshire village of Hucknall Torkard. One of the witnesses at the wedding was Humphry Davy (Daff) Hudson who represented the Hudson family of Bakewell. By 1901 young William and his wife, Mabel, were living at Mabel's father's house in Hucknall Torkard with their seven year old son who was yet another William Greaves!

After the death of Billy Greaves in 1894 his widow, Ellen, with the support of various nephews and nieces from the Allsop side of her family, continued to run The Rutland Arms and Haddon Farm for about 12 months. She then retired to Great Longstone where she lived at The Lodge with a sister, a cousin and a niece.

Also in 1894, on 6th September, Will Hudson married his second wife, Mary Isabel Lowe, the daughter of yet another hotel keeper from Little Longstone. She soon gave birth to a daughter, Kate. Known as Katie, she later married Tom Sheppard who came from a family who worked as painters and decorators in Bakewell for several generations from the shop on the corner of Bridge Street just in front of the Castle Hotel.

Tourists began to pour into Bakewell by train, coach and, more fashionably, by bicycle. Will encouraged parties of cyclists to visit the town and The Castle became the headquarters of the local branch of the Cyclist Touring Club (CTC). The hotel was also the scene of several property auctions, boasted a billiard room, and had a photographers' darkroom on the premises.

In 1896 Will and Mary had another daughter who was baptised Mary, but was always known as 'Mollie'. She later married the 'boy next door', George Smith. The Smith family literally lived in the house next door to the Castle Hotel in Castle Street. George's father, Robert Smith, later owned Rutland Works, better known in Bakewell as Smith's wood yard, which firstly George and Mollie Smith and then afterwards, their son Clifford Hudson Smith and his family, ran successfully for many years. The buildings in the wood-yard are now owned by a local architect (who was a member of my patrol in the Boy Scouts in the late 1950s) and they have been converted into very attractive apartments. Much of the land around the wood yard, including the allotments where cousin John Hudson grew his dahlias, have been converted into successful car park schemes still owned by Will and Mary Hudson's descendents.

60 YEAR OLD KING EDWARD VII
EVENTUALLY FOLLOWS HIS MUM, 1901

My Grandad, Will Hudson, the landlord of the Castle & Commercial Hotel, would soon be destined to become a widower again. In 1903, when their daughters, Katie and Mollie, were aged only eight and six respectively, his wife, Mary, died of a cerebral haemorrhage leaving Will to bring up his three young daughters from his two short-lived marriages.

Will was an accomplished horse rider and would often ride as far as the Newhaven Inn to visit a friend. He was one of the first in Bakewell to own and drive a motor car. Will and his best friend at the time, Scotsman Johnny Waddell, used to tour the locality in their new automobiles as far as the poor quality of the roads in the district would permit. Johnny Waddell lodged with the Smith family in Castle Street next door to the Castle Hotel and was the general manager of the new DP (Dujardin-planté) Battery Co. Ltd. at Lumford Mills, built on the site of Richard Arkwright's old cotton mill of 1778. The DP manufactured large electric storage batteries for submarines, hospitals, cinemas and other large public buildings and vehicles. Waddell was the first general manager of the DP and my father, Gill Hudson, was the general manager when the company sadly closed down in 1970.

Will Hudson photographed around the time he married my Granny, Annie Marples, in 1905.
[Hudson Collection]

Will was a keen cricketer and played for Bakewell CC for many years before donning the umpire's coat. Following in his father's footsteps, he was a senior member of the Dorothy Vernon Masonic Lodge and was a delegate to the Derbyshire Licensed Victuallers Association. He was the Secretary of the Bakewell & District Boy Scouts Association and an honorary member of the Bakewell Conservative Club.

Will used his contacts in the LVA again, only this time to find a third wife. On this occasion he went to Eyam, the 'Plague Village' where he found the lady who was destined to become my Granny, who was helping her brother, Jack Marples, to run the Miners' Arms. Their father, William Marples, had been the landlord of the Miners' for almost 50 years but he had died just a few months before the wedding. Jack Marples remained the licensee of the Miners' until 1934 and many of his descendants still live in Eyam today.

The young lady he found in Eyam was Annie Marples and Will married her in September 1905 in Eyam Parish Church. Together, they were to run the Castle Hotel in Bakewell for the next 12 years.

Although my Grandad Will already had three daughters, the eldest of which was nearly 20, he was obviously very keen to produce a son and heir! To his great pleasure and relief in 1907, Annie gave birth to a son, William (always known as Bill). A daughter, Annie (known as Betty) was born in 1908; after a slight breather for my Granny Annie there followed John (known as Jack) in 1911; my father, Gilbert (known as Gill) in 1912; and finally Harriet (known as Hearty) in 1913. All five of Will and Annie's children were born at the Castle Hotel.

In 1915 Will retired from the Castle Hotel and took his family to 'Wood View', a house in Granby Croft by the River Wye. In an advertisement a few years earlier Wood View had boasted an entrance hall, dining room, sitting room, kitchen, pantry, scullery, four bedrooms, a store-room and a coal place. It also had hot and cold water and the annual rent was at that time just £20! That same house has been lived in continuously by members of the Hudson family for well over 90 years and, at the time of writing, is occupied by the families of two of Will's grandsons.

Will Hudson on the front step of the Castle Hotel c.1911 with his daughters, Mollie (later Smith) and Katie (later Sheppard) risking the traffic in Bridge Street. [Hudson Collection]

TIME FOR A CHANGE! FROM HOUSE OF SAXE-COBURG-GOTHA TO HOUSE OF WINDSOR, 1917

Will Hudson worked for the Ministry of Food during the last years of World War I and into the early 1920s. In her fascinating diary of the period from 1913 to 1920, Maria Gyte, the landlady of the Devonshire Arms in the village of Sheldon, near Bakewell, wrote that on 16th July 1918: *"Showery first thing then a thunderstorm and heavier rain, close. Mr Hudson [Food Office, Bakewell] called and asked a few questions about 4 penny beer and cards relating to supplying meals."* On 17th May 1920 she wrote: *"Anthony [her husband] took the new mare in float to market. He bought a barren cow and lying off calves. He called to see Mr Hudson about the spirits and beer prices."*

Will's younger brother, Humphry Davy (Daff), was the manager of Williams Deacon's Bank in Bakewell for many years in the magnificent building built in 1838 that overlooks The Square. At the time of writing, that same building houses the Royal Bank of Scotland. His spacious apartments above the bank and garden at the back – now part of Bath Gardens – were often the scene of Hudson family parties. After having been manager of the bank in Snitterton Road, Matlock, for several years, Daff eventually retired from banking to live in Hathersage.

Another of Will's brothers, Gilbert James, was the chief accountant in the Duke of Devonshire's Estate Office in Buxton. He was also a member of the Derbyshire Special Constabulary in Buxton and was a prolific batsman for Buxton Cricket Club. The fourth brother, Charles Greaves Hudson worked for the Inland Revenue.

Grandad Will with my Granny Annie, brother Roger and myself at their home at Wood View, Granby Croft in 1948. [Hudson Collection]

Will Hudson lived on Granby Croft with his third wife, Annie, and family until 1953 when he died at the age of 88 years.

Will's eldest son, Bill, worked for a time at the DP Battery Co. Ltd. before taking over the license of the Wheatsheaf Hotel in Bakewell from the parents of his wife, Jan Wilson in 1946; Betty married farmer, Len Mosley, and lived at Birchills Farm on the Chatsworth Estate; Jack, who remained single, worked for Mouldensite Ltd of Darley Dale, which later became Bakelite Ltd and on relocation took him to London; my Dad, Gill, joined the DP Battery from school and worked his way up to become General Manager; Hearty, who also remained single, was a WREN during World War II before becoming the formidable receptionist for dentists John Batty & Allan Eaton in Rutland Chambers, Bakewell.

"L" TYPE.

Type usually supplied.

"LC" TYPE.

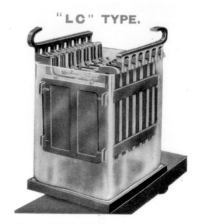

This type is fitted with our special binding clamps
to facilitate erection.

Three inches clearance between plates and bottom of box.

Suitable for Private Plants, Institutions, &c.,

with Ordinary Rates of Charge and Discharge.

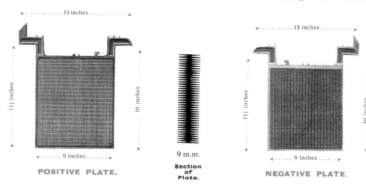

POSITIVE PLATE.

Section of Plate. 9 m.m.

NEGATIVE PLATE.

These cells are made in accordance with the very latest and most efficient practice, and are of the hanging type, with cast Planté positives of enormous surface with skin formation, the plates being suspended upon the sides of the glass boxes, and are designed to meet the demand for a cell of this type, combined with the simplicity of handling for erection and low price of our Strip Type.

LUMFORD MILLS, BAKEWELL, DERBYSHIRE.

Left: DP leaflet showing smoky chimneys and the waterwheel.
Above: DP leaflet showing some of the early batteries they produced.

[Hudson Collection]

Bill's children all stayed in the Bakewell area. John was the groundsman at St. Anselm's School; Geoff was a builder and for a time was the steward at Matlock Golf Club; June was a nurse who married the Duke of Rutland's comptroller at Haddon Hall; Billy was a carpenter who managed his father's pub, The Wheatsheaf, for many years; and Mary worked at the Westminster Bank. Needless to say, from time to time they all helped their parents to run The Wheatsheaf or The 'Sheaf' as it is locally known.

Betty's son, Brian, was a farmer and emigrated to Australia; Tricia married the owner of Bakewell's R Orme & Co Ltd, the 'Peak' family grocers and wine merchants which had operated in The Square in Bakewell, in Crown Square, Matlock, and in outlying villages from the 1880s; younger daughter, Gill married the owner of Riber Hall Hotel, near Matlock.

My brother, Roger, spent a lifetime in the hotel trade and managed hotels all around the country. My sister, Jane, was for a time the receptionist at Bakewell Medical Centre before she married and moved away from the town.

My Dad, Gill Hudson, left school and went straight to work for DP Battery at Lumford Mill. He took a full part in Bakewell life and was a member of the Parish Church choir, the Bakewell Orpheus Operatic and Dramatic Society, and in his spare time he helped at Bakewell Library when it was located in the Market Hall. He was a life-long member of the Boy Scout movement as scout, Scout Master and later as District Commissioner. He was also a Churchwarden at Bakewell Church for many years.

Dad's greatest love was sport. He was able to play most sports with great skill and competitiveness. His headmaster at Lady Manners School, Ian P Macdonald, told him that one day he would probably play rugby for England. Dad did eventually play for England, but not at rugby!

Reg Harvey was the senior master at Lady Manners School and taught both Dad and myself. He was known as 'Fig' to both staff and children at the school. In his wonderful book 'The Story of the School of Grace, Lady Manners, Bakewell' Reg related how Mr McDonald introduced rugby to the school in March 1926. I am sorry to have to prove 'Fig' wrong after all these years but I have a photograph of Dad in the Lady Manners School Rugby 1st XV of **1925**. He was 13 at the time and played at scrum-half.

Dad was captain of the School Rugby 1st XV and Cricket 1st XI in 1928. He played rugby for the Old Mannerians 1st XV in their inaugural match in 1929. His collar-bone was broken playing for them and in his first rugby match back after injury he broke his wrist! Granny Hudson told him in no uncertain terms that he was never to play rugby again! Not to be completely defeated he went straight down to The Recreation Ground from his home in Granby Croft and asked the players of the local hockey team if he could join in.

Lady Manners School Rugby 1st XV of 1925 with Dad, cross-legged on the right, at the age of 13! [Hudson Collection]

Lady Manners School Cricket 1st XI of 1925 with Dad, cross-legged on the right still aged 13! [Hudson Collection]

Back row: brother-in-law, Len Mosley, far left; brother, Jack, centre wearing spectacles; Gill, far right.

Bakewell Hockey Club in The Rec c1931. [Hudson Collection]

Front row: Fred Pidcock, far left; brother, Bill, far right.

Dad played for Bakewell Hockey Club from that day, his position being right-back. He first appeared for Derbyshire Hockey Club in 1931, aged 19, and played for the county until 1952, many times as captain.

He had his first trial for the Midland Counties Hockey Club in 1932 and represented them from 1937 to 1951, several times captaining the side. He played for the Derwent Hockey Club from 1935 until 1952, most years as their captain.

Dad played cricket for Bakewell Cricket Club and Old Mannerians Cricket Club throughout the 1930s, often playing alongside his two elder brothers, Bill & Jack. He captained the OMCC in 1937 and was a stylish batsman and reliable wicket keeper.

On 24th July 1935 he was chosen to play cricket for Derbyshire Club & Ground XI at Clay Cross, the first of several outings for the team.

In 1948 Dad was selected to be a member of the Great Britain Hockey Squad that won the silver medal in the Olympic Games in London.

HOCKEY WORLD, Friday, February 18, 1938.

HOCKEY WORLD

Also incorporating HOCKEY and HOCKEY ILLUSTRATED.

CIRCULATING THROUGHOUT THE UNITED KINGDOM AND OVERSEAS.

(THE OFFICIAL AND NATIONAL ORGAN OF THE GAME IN GREAT BRITAIN AND IRELAND)

EDITED BY E. A. C. THOMSON

Vol. XVI. No. 21. FRIDAY, FEBRUARY 18, 1938. PRICE FOURPENCE

INDEX TO PRINCIPAL CONTENTS:

The Week's Personality.

No. XXI.—A MIDLAND AND DERBYSHIRE FULL-BACK.

MR. GILL HUDSON, who gained his colours for the Midlands this season in the two English trials, was educated at Lady Manners School, Bakewell. He obtained his colours for Rugby and cricket and captained both teams in 1938. When he left school, he became a member of the Old Mannerian R.F.C. and played at scrum half. Unfortunately, he sustained a broken wrist and collar bone in successive matches. This compelled him to cease playing with the oval ball and consider the question of hockey.

He commenced the stick game in 1929 with the Bakewell H.C., but subsequently joined the Derwent H.C. in 1935. Mr. Hudson was chosen for Derbyshire at right full back in 1931, a position he has occupied ever since. Altogether he has appeared thirty-eight times for the county to date, and is likely to continue to hold this position for a further considerable period.

GILL HUDSON (Midlands).

Included in the first Midland trial in 1932, he also figured in the preliminary Midland trial in 1936. This year, Mr. Hudson has taken part in both Midland trials v. North and Combined Services respectively at right back and left back.

It was owing to the indisposition of Mr. R. F. Barnes, the Warwickshire back, that Mr. Hudson was called upon to take his place against the North at Nottingham. His form was sufficiently convincing to create confidence amongst the Midland selectors. He was invited again to play, and

did so play against the Combined Services at Portsmouth.

Steadiness in defence is Mr. Hudson's special characteristic; a sure and sound tackler and hits the ball with strength and crispness. Naturally, his county and his club were delighted at his success which was an honour for them as well as for himself.

Mr. Hudson is a consistent and regular member of the Derbyshire Rams, a Sunday club, and a stalwart in their defence. His other sports are Badminton, cricket and lawn tennis, a combination which seems to be popular nowadays with so many hockey players.

He was the captain of the Old Mannerian Cricket eleven in 1937, and finished up with an average of 35, rather good going, and shewing that he is as skilful with the bat as he is with the stick.

That he should have already made thirty-eight appearances for Derbyshire shews the county selection committee have confidence in his ability. It is more than likely that Mr. Hudson will continue to wear the county colours for a much longer spell.

Both for his club and county, Mr. Hudson's success in getting into the Midland trial teams this season has created immense satisfaction. It will be a sure encouragement to him another season to get further in the playing limelight of Midland representative hockey.

" ARGUS."

Above: 'Hockey World' article featuring Gill Hudson, dated 18th February 1938.

Opposite Top: Gill Hudson, sitting cross-legged on the far right, with the Great Britain Hockey Squad - Olympic Games 1948. [Hudson Collection]

Opposite Bottom: Gill, back row 4th from left, in the England line-up to play Wales at Abergavenny on 26th March 1949. [Hudson Collection]

There is a wonderful letter in existence from Dad to Jessie Nadin, his boss at the DP Battery Company, written on 13th September 1948. Dad informed Mr Nadin that he had been selected to represent the Great Britain hockey team in their forthcoming fixture against Holland in Amsterdam. He then explained that he was willing to use up his last day of holiday leave in order to play in the match. Mr Nadin's reply contained congratulations on his selection and said that he should accept the offer. The proviso was that, whilst he was in Amsterdam, Dad had to find time to meet one of the DP's clients in Holland who had recently complained about the quality of a truck battery bought from the factory!!

Dad played several times for Great Britain and the England Hockey team from 1947 to 1949. His headmaster's prediction about him playing for England was correct - well almost!! He retired from hockey in 1952.

Gill married my mother, Marjorie Rogers, in 1941. Mum's father, Iley James Rogers, was the owner of a knitting factory in Manchester. During the First World War 'I.J.', as he was known, opened the Progress Works Knitting Factory in Buxton Road, Bakewell, on the site of the Chesterfield Brewery Co. stores. This building had formerly been the Commercial Inn built by Richard Arkwright in 1827 and had also been known as The New Inn and The Roebuck. The building is now a block of flats called Progress House.

Mum (Marjorie Rogers) c1935.
[Hudson Collection]

Dad c1935.
[Hudson Collection]

On 31st October 1921 Princess Mary, The Princess Royal, visited Progress Works whilst on a visit to the Duke and Duchess of Devonshire at Chatsworth. My mother, aged five, accompanied her father during the visit and presented Princess Mary with a bouquet of flowers.

In 1924 my Grandpa, I J Rogers, was the President of the Bakewell Hospital Demonstration Committee, and as such, suggested that essential funds could be raised for local hospitals by holding a carnival in Bakewell. He formed the Carnival Committee which has been responsible for organising the Bakewell Carnival ever since. 'I.J.' was also the first President of the Bakewell Orpheus Operatic and Dramatic Society.

My mother, Marjorie, aged 5, has just presented a bouquet of flowers to Princess Mary, The Princess Royal, on the occasion of a Royal Visit by her to my Grandpa Rogers' knitting factory in Buxton Road on 31st October 1921. Grandpa is also in the photograph. [Hudson Collection]

An aerial photograph of the DP Battery Co Ltd taken in 1939 showing the waterwheel to the left of the front chimney and my first house, Bankside, at the bottom of the image. [Hudson Collection]

My Dad was devastated when, in 1970, the D P Battery Co. Ltd. was forced to close down. For many years as General Manager he had selflessly campaigned to prevent the company's closure, meeting and negotiating with government ministers and trade union leaders time after time but all to no avail. He was unable to comprehend why the factory in Bakewell was to be closed when it was operating in profit and two larger companies within the same group – at Clifton near Manchester and at Dagenham in Essex – were allowed to survive when neither of them was profitable. He was very conscious of the terrible effect the loss of 300 good jobs would be on the small population of Bakewell. He worked tirelessly to help all his workforce to find new employment, some being relocated to jobs as far away as South Africa and Australia. He encouraged Fearnehough's – a small tool manufacturing company from Sheffield – to take over the main site of the factory and many of his former employees were able to find employment with the new company. He filled the smaller buildings with new enterprises like Pinelog Ltd, a flourishing company which is still part of the Riverside Business Park.

Following his retirement Dad's favourite pastime was trout fishing in the small reservoir behind the DP Battery factory known as the DP Dam. It stored water to drive the waterwheel and power the factory right up to the 1950s. I can remember spending hours watching the wheel splashing round and round when I lived on Lumford. I could hear the noise of the wheel from my bedroom window. The reservoir was emptied many years ago for safety reasons.

Dad died in 1994 after a lifetime in Bakewell. Mum pre-deceased him by 10 months.

The author, father Gill, and brother Roger at Bakewell, July 14th 1985. [Hudson Collection]

I was born at The Croft Nursing Home in Buxton in July 1947 and was baptised and later confirmed at All Saint's Church in Bakewell. I lived first at Bankside, a DP Battery property on Lumford, and later at The Crest, which was my Grandpa Rogers' former house up Yeld Road in Bakewell.

After several years at Mrs Sands' kindergarten school held at Holme Hall in Bakewell I attended Woodlands Preparatory School in Matlock. I then followed many of my Hudson ancestors to Lady Manners Grammar School in Bakewell.

I also followed in Dad's footsteps by playing rugby for the Old Mannerians RFC and cricket for Bakewell CC. I was even in the Old Mannerians Rugby Club cricket team that won the coveted Stanley Orme Shield in 1964, a knockout cricket competition for local clubs. My cousin, Patricia Orme, the wife of the sponsor, presented me with my winner's trophy at the end of the match. We defeated Bakewell CC in the nail-biting final, Hudson cousins and all!

Back row: Ged Tracy, Geoff Henson, Derek Ramsden, Trevor Gratton, Mick Marvin, Robert Parker.

Front row: John Hart, Alan Briggs, Peter Bennett, Bob Winthrop, Myself.

Old Mannerians RFC cricket team which beat Bakewell CC in the final of the Stanley Orme Shield Knockout Cup in 1964. [Hudson Collection]

At the age of 17 I joined the Metropolitan Police Cadet Corps and went to the Police Training School at Hendon. At 19 I became a police constable and was posted to West End Central Police Station which had the responsibility for policing the whole of Soho and Mayfair. At 21 I applied for and was accepted by the Special Branch at Scotland Yard and enjoyed an exciting and varied career.

57

Rugby was my great love and during my rugby career I represented the Metropolitan Police, Bishop's Stortford, Trojans and Hampshire County XVs, as well as the Old Mannerians RFC. Although I retired from rugby many years ago I still play squash regularly and the occasional game of cricket.

At the time of my retirement from the police force in 1996 I was based at 10 Downing Street where I was second-in-command of Prime Minister John Major's personal protection team. In the course of my years working with him I was fortunate enough to travel to over 55 countries of the world, many of them on several occasions.

Each summer, much to my intense enjoyment, we were very regular visitors to all the English Test Match cricket grounds! I was lucky enough to rub shoulders with many amazing cricket personalities spanning several generations.

Back row: Dixie Broome, John Pearce, Terry Green & Geoff Henson

Front row: Myself, Trevor Gratton & Brian Hoole

Old Mannerians RFC – Derbyshire Seven-a-side Champions in 1963. [Hudson Collection]

Since I retired I have lived with my family in idyllic seclusion in North Cornwall where we run a small holiday business – yes, even my wife and I, like so many of our relatives, provide accommodation and sustenance for our visitors, although no alcohol! The Hudson family seems, one way or the other, to have been heavily involved in entertaining for so many generations – from the end of the 1700s, and possibly even earlier, right up to the present time.

My daughter, Alice, in the Great Hall at Chequers, with John Major – New Year's Eve, 1993.
[Hudson Collection]

Boris Yeltsin, myself and John Major coming out of 10 Downing Street – May 1994.
[Hudson Collection]

BAKEWELL PUDDING

The Bakewell Pudding has made the town of Bakewell famous the world over. The pudding was originated by my great-great-great-grandmother, Mrs Ann Greaves. It is generally accepted that some time in the early 1800s she asked one of her cooks to make a dish to be served as a dessert in the dining room of The Rutland Arms. The cook made a slight mistake with the ingredients, the customers thought the dessert was very tasty, Mrs Greaves shrewdly made a note of the amended recipe, and the Bakewell Pudding which became a speciality of the inn was born. She kept the details of the recipe a very closely guarded secret and handed them down through the family before she died. The actual dishes in which she cooked the Bakewell Puddings are also still held within the family.

Mrs Isabella Beeton included two different versions of a Bakewell Pudding recipe in her famous Family Cookbook published in 1859.

Of course, in the 1960s Mr Kipling introduced a cake covered with icing and mounted by a cherry. He called it a Cherry Bakewell Tart! The reaction of many older members of my family to his creation was to remind me that the only tarts to be seen in Bakewell were usually to be found slinking around the bus shelter in Rutland Square opposite The Rutland on a Saturday evening! I'm sure the town has changed a lot since then!

Mrs Greaves left her recipe to her Hudson and Greaves descendents when she died in 1866 and it is a tradition within the Hudson family that each new wife at a wedding involving one of the family receives her own copy of Mrs Greaves' original Bakewell Pudding recipe for her own use.

One legend states that a Mr James Radford of Castle Street drew up Mrs Greaves' will and somehow the recipe came into his possession. This story quickly loses credibility as records show that when Mrs Greaves retired from The Rutland and moved to Manchester, Mr Radford would only have been just 5 years old, and when she died in 1866 he would have been only 15 years old!

A Mrs Wilson started selling a version of the Bakewell Pudding from her shop in Rutland Square. This shop is now known as The Old Original Bakewell Pudding Shop. However, my Grandad, Will Hudson, decided to introduce a little healthy competition into the town when he gave his good friend, George Bloomer, a copy of Mrs Greaves' own Bakewell Pudding recipe. This allowed George to boast that *"G E Bloomer Ltd of Matlock Street, Bakewell"*, were *"Makers of the Celebrated Bakewell Pudding from the Original Recipe"*.

As a reward for giving George Bloomer full access to his great-grandmother's recipe Grandad Will was provided with a free loaf of bread from Bloomer's Shop in Matlock Street for the rest of his life. This was quite some remuneration when you consider that my Grandad lived until 1953 and reached the grand old age of 88!

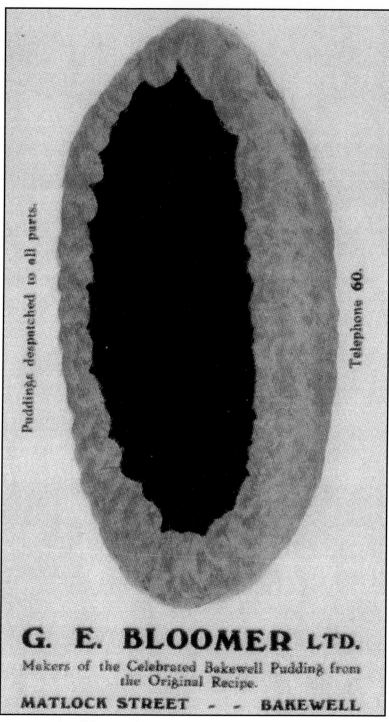

A well-known advertisement for George Bloomer's shop

61

CONCLUSION

Well, there it is – the full story of Mrs Ann Greaves and her family together with a few tales about some of her descendants, many of them innkeepers, hoteliers, and publicans. Yes, Sir Joseph Paxton and George Stephenson were related to the family by marriage. No, Sir Humphry Davy was not a relative but to retrace his close association with Ann's first son, James Hudson, you would have thought he was! James quite obviously idolised Davy and he would have been more than thrilled to know that since the 1830s there have been six generations of Hudsons who have been christened 'Humphry Davy'. There are currently several boys and men in the family with the first name 'Davy' and there is still at least one 'James Hudson' who was born in 1997!

We should not forget The Rutland Arms which still towers over Rutland Square. It is the meeting place for locals and visitors alike and holds so much of the history of Bakewell within its walls (and cellars!). For almost the whole of the nineteenth century the innkeepers were either Hudson's or Greaves' but most importantly they were related to Mrs Ann Greaves.

Bakewell has changed a lot over the years, more so since the days of my childhood in the 1950s. It has become more popular with day-trippers from the surrounding cities as well as those who stay in the many accommodation providers and walk and cycle around the Peak District. I hardly recognise the shops of my youth. I remember when my Auntie Jeanne Rogers' café, 'Byways' in Water Lane, was the only café in Bakewell! How Bakewell has moved on since then!

Mrs Greaves certainly wouldn't recognise Bakewell nowadays and she probably wouldn't recognise the Bakewell Puddings being served up in the town either! However, I'm sure she would be very content to think that she played such an enormous part in the future prosperity and popularity of the town by creating the first Bakewell Pudding all those years ago and by passing it down for all to enjoy. She certainly put Bakewell on the map!

I have managed to trace approximately 350-400 descendents of James & Ann Hudson, the first innkeepers of The Rutland Arms. The list increases weekly! One was killed in action in World War I and another lost his life in the 2nd World War. Two other members of the family regrettably committed suicide. One married a politician in Mrs Thatcher's government and her husband subsequently received a knighthood.

I know that many of James and Ann's descendants still live in the Bakewell area. As well as many Hudsons there are family members with the following surnames still living in the locality. I apologise if I have missed any off the list: Bettney, Biggin, Boot, Button, Davis, Greaves, Fisher, Hodgkinson, Hooton, Hutson, Lilley, Mann, Marriott, Massey, Mosley, Orme, Pearson, Sheppard, Sigley, Simons, Smith, Swanwick, Tibbles, Turner, Webster, Whitaker, White, Wilson.